PENGUINS

PENGUINS

ROBIN NAGLE

GALLERY BOOKS

An Imprint of W.H. Smith
Publishers Inc.
112 Madison Avenue
New York, New York 10016

The publisher would like to
thank Dr. Christine Sheppard for her assistance.

A FRIEDMAN GROUP BOOK

Published by GALLERY BOOKS
An imprint of W.H. Smith Publishers, Inc.
112 Madison Avenue
New York, New York 10016

ISBN 0-8317-6792-8

PENGUINS
was prepared and produced by
Michael Friedman Publishing Group, Inc.
15 West 26th Street
New York, NY 10010

Editor: Sharyn Rosart
Art Director: Robert W. Kosturko
Designer: Deborah Kaplan
Photography Editor: Christopher Bain
Production: Karen L. Greenberg

Typeset by Mar + x Myles Typographic Services
Color separation by Universal Colour Scanning, Ltd.
Printed and bound in Hong Kong by Leefung Asco Printers Ltd.

Gallery Books are available for bulk purchase for sales
promotions and premium use. For details write or telephone the
Manager of Special Sales. W.H. Smith Publishers, Inc., 112
Madison Avenue, New York, New York 10016. (212) 532-6600.

Dedication

This book is dedicated to my uncle,

Charles L. Nagle,

whose wisdom, gentle spirit,

and compassion for the natural world

have been a continual source

of guidance.

About the Author

Robin Nagle is a free-lance science

and general-interest writer living

in New York City.

Contents

Introduction

Penguins have been called nature's best dressed birds. They are certainly among the best loved. Penguin likenesses adorn corporate logos, zoo and aquarium emblems, comic strips, wrapping paper, jewelry, calendars, mugs—the list is endless. But who are the real penguins? Do they wear black-and-white tuxedos? Where do they live? How many penguins are there? How many kinds of penguins are there? Do they all live in cold climates? How do they stay warm? Scientists have been investigating these questions for decades. While they don't know everything there is to know about penguins, they have discovered a large amount of fascinating information. For example, we know today that the biggest penguin in the world is the emperor penguin, at sixty pounds (twenty-seven kg); the smallest is the fairy penguin, at about a pound and a half (less than one kilogram).

Penguin habitats cover a good portion of the globe, ranging from the coldest to the hottest climates. Some penguins look like the stereotype, with bold two-color feathering. Others show a bluish

*T*he
**Falkland Islands are home
to these yellow-marked
king penguins.**
. . . .

color. One species has yellow eyes. Yet others have plumes that spring so zanily from their heads and are such a bold yellow color that one wonders if they inspired contemporary punk hairstyles.

But much about penguins remains a mystery. In fact, there's even disagreement about exactly how many species of penguins there are. Some sources say there are eighteen distinct species, but others argue there are only seventeen. And there's yet a third body of opinion that argues for sixteen species.

Most penguin habitats are known; it's not hard to see penguins on the ground when they're gathered in colonies of thousands, even millions. But when the birds are at sea, where do they go? How far do they swim? How do penguins know how to return each year, generation after generation, to the place they were born? And how long have extant rookeries, or nesting grounds, existed? Significant penguin fossils have been found in sites that are still used by contemporary colonies. Is it possible that some penguin rookeries are millions of years old?

This book won't answer great unsolved penguin mysteries. Not even the world's premiere penguin researchers can do that yet. It will give the reader an introduction to the stout, waddling birds that have intrigued humans for generations. If you already like penguins, you'll like them more. If you don't know them well, you'll know them better. And if you can't stand penguins—perhaps you're like the observer who said penguins look like "animated laundry bags"—you're about to meet a group of creatures whose unique physiology and startling diversity has much to offer bird researchers, bird lovers, and students of nature.

CHAPTER 1

HUMANS MEET PENGUINS

The first people who encountered penguins were the people who live where penguins live. The Maori of New Zealand no doubt knew their penguin neighbors and probably dined on them. Some Africans living at the tip of the continent also knew the penguins that lived nearby, though there are no written records of Maori- or African-penguin contact. And in the South Atlantic, from the southernmost inhabited region of Tierra del Fuego to the rocky coasts of Chile and the cliffs of Argentina, penguins were a source of food, skins, tools, and perhaps oil.

The rest of the world, however, didn't know about penguins until Europe's Age of Exploration sent navigators far south.

*A*délies'
feathers cover more of
their beaks and feet than
any other bird in the world
(above). The extra
feathering helps protect
them from the
Antarctic cold.

. . . .

A lone
penguin (right) is
rare. This gentoo could be
vulnerable to predators if
he or she is separated from
the colony.

. . . .

*I*cebergs
(opposite page) are giant
chips off glaciers; some may
be quite ancient.

. . . .

FIRST RECORDED DISCOVERIES

Penguins live only in the southern hemisphere, as far north as the equator and as far south as the Antarctic. European explorers, seeing penguins for the first time, used names for already familiar species of similar size and coloration, such as auks and geese, when they recorded their observations. The origin of the word "penguin" is not known.

Penguins have fascinated people in the northern hemisphere ever since Portuguese navigator Vasco da Gama brought home reports of strange birds off the tip of South Africa that "bray like asses." In records from his voyage of 1497, he called the birds *sotilicarios,* a name previously given to great auks from much farther north. Da Gama and his crew probably saw what today are called black-footed, or "jackass" penguins (*Spheniscus demersus*). As their name implies, these African birds have black feet and a call that resembles that of a donkey.

In 1520, another Portuguese expedition, this one guided by Ferdinand Magellan, brought home reports of odd birds off the tip of South America. The Magellan expedition carried an Italian passenger named Antonio Pigafetta who kept a detailed diary of the trip. He reported the discovery of two islands "full of geese and goslings . . . [they] are black and have feathers over their whole body of the same size and fashion, and they do not fly, and they live on fish." It is not known exactly which two islands were home to these birds, although some suggest they were off the coast of Patagonia, or southern Argentina. Pigafetta's "geese" were very likely penguins. Appropriately, they're called Magellanic penguins today (*Spheniscus magellanicus*). The rookery, or penguin colony, that Pigafetta sighted may still thrive.

The English followed Magellan in 1578, with Francis Drake's expedition around South America. Patagonia proved a good place to penguin-watch. Like his Portuguese predecessor, Drake recorded an odd flock of birds, "a great store of foule which could not flie, of the bigness of geese." Drake noted that the birds, not yet called penguins, tasted "not farre unlike a fat goose in England."

The first known use of the word *penguin* occurred in the late 1850s. A member of Thomas Cavendish's crew reported that when sailing off the coast of Patagonia, they "killed and salted a great store of Penguins for victuals." They called a nearby island Penguin Island, the name it still bears today.

Captain James Cook's famous world voyage in the mid-1770s included Johann Reinhold Forster among the crew. Forster was one of the first scientists to offer detailed descriptions of penguins. The scientific name of the emperor penguin, *Aptenodytes forsteri*, was given in honor of Forster.

*B*lackfooted
penguins (right) are the
only penguins that live off
the tip of South Africa.

*B*elow, a
drawing of an Adélie
penguin. Adélies have the
classic black-and-white
tuxedo markings most
people associate with
penguins.

A French voyage of 1837–40 resulted in another penguin name. The expedition was led by Jules Sebastien César Dumont d'Urville. He named a vast expanse of the Antarctic Adélie Land after his wife. One of the penguin species that lives there is called, appropriately, the Adélie (*Pygoscelis adeliae*). Adélies are the best-known penguins, the kind featured in cartoons and artists' depictions of the "typical" penguin.

When explorers across the centuries returned home with news of penguins and assorted other aquatic beasts, European's weren't slow to realize the potential profit offered by those animals. Ships set sail for the Antarctic and nearby waters to hunt whales, seals, and penguins. In 1858, sealers on Heard Island found king penguins a convenient source of clothing, and the birds' blubber provided fuel for cooking and keeping warm.

Later, king penguin blubber was used to make roof-sealing oil. Sealers and whalers waited until the birds came to shore to mate and nest, then drove them by the thousands into huge oil cookers.

Off the coast of South Africa, 300,000 black-footed penguin eggs were sold every year. Penguin eggs were a regular part of the diet of Falkland Islanders until relatively recently. The egg harvesting was particularly devastating for the Falkland king penguins. Even though such harvesting has been strictly controlled for decades, there are only four small colonies of king penguins left in the Falklands, and it will take a long time for their numbers to return to the levels of pre-harvesting days.

Another area of jeopardy for penguins comes from a surprising source. Scientists have been a regular part of the penguin landscape since the early 1900s, but it wasn't until the 1950s that they began to realize their presence was detrimental to penguins' mating and breeding habits. Researchers from the Palmer Station on the Antarctic Peninsula have noted declines in the Adélie population on Torgerson Island, where Palmer Station workers frequently visit. Chin strap (*Pygoscelis antarctica*) and gentoo (*Pygoscelis papua*) penguin populations at Waterboat Point have grown smaller; these penguins are regularly studied by scientists working out of the nearby Chilean research station, Gonzalez Videla. Never-

theless, scientists' negative impact on penguins is far less than that of overfishing, pollution, and ozone depletion.

Tourists have been another bothersome element, and it's no wonder: adventurers who explored the Antarctic in the 1920s and '30s brag about walking right into a penguin rookery and sitting down amidst thousands of breeding birds or newly hatched chicks.

Today, all penguin habitats are protected, and there is no mass exploitation of penguins for their feathers, skin, meat, eggs, or blubber. It doesn't mean penguins are completely safe from human activity, but it is a start.

*T*his engraving (left) shows part of D'Urville's crew landing at Adélie Land.

READING THE RECORD OF THE PAST

In general, birds are not well represented in the fossil record. This holds true for penguins, too, but enough evidence has been unearthed to give us some solid clues about the penguin past.

The first fossil penguin was found in New Zealand in a limestone quarry in the late 1850s. No one in New Zealand knew what it was, so they sent it to London to be examined by the renowned scientist Thomas Henry Huxley. Penguin bone structure is similar to other birds, but penguins have one bone found in no other bird. The New Zealand fossil included this bone providing certain evidence that the fossil was indeed that of a penguin.

Penguin fossils were found in Australia in the late 1880s, and on Seymour Island near the Antarctic in the early 1900s. In South America, fossil remains were found in about 1890. South African penguin fossils weren't discovered until 1970. The South American fossils are the largest collection; most of them have been found on the coast of Patagonia, near where Pigafetta sighted the strange "geese."

Many ancient penguins were larger than their contemporary counterparts. The penguins that left behind New Zealand fossils, and most other ancestral penguins, reached about five feet (1.5 meters) in height. The biggest fossil penguin was *Anthropornis nordenskjoeldi*, found in Seymour Island near the Antarctic. It stood an average of five feet four inches (1.6 meters) and weighed about 300 pounds (135 kilograms). In comparison, the largest living penguin is the emperor, which stands roughly four feet (1.2 meters) and weighs about sixty pounds (twenty-seven kilograms).

Galapagos penguins (left) are the most tropical penguins, living near the equator in the Galapagos Islands.

A summer's day on an Antarctic "beach" for this group of Adélies (opposite page).

Penguins probably evolved from airborne ancestors about 65 million years ago, and the eighteen species we know today probably started to differentiate from a common source about 55 million years ago. The dates are speculative, however, since no fossils have been found from the Cretaceous or Paleocene eras, when these changes are supposed to have occurred.

The oldest penguin remains date back 45 million years. Even that long ago, the fossils indicate that some penguin development was highly specialized and that ancient penguins had mostly the same adaptations and behavior as today's penguins. Interestingly, all known penguin fossils have been found in locations that still have penguin populations. That indicates that at least some penguin rookeries are incredibly old.

Some researchers contend that there were more penguin species of yore than there are today, and that some were even more specialized. This may mean that there have been

many more species of penguin across time than the ones we know today. Unfortunately, many of these species lived on land that no longer exists, so the chances of finding their fossilized remains are slim.

Related fossil evidence suggests that the sea and air in which ancient penguins lived was much warmer than today's Antarctic, though some modern species do breed in warmer waters. Researchers have found fossilized remains of plants and animals that couldn't have survived in today's frigid climate but that apparently did well in a warmer ancient era.

Because today's penguins do not fly, some people mistakenly think they are primitive birds. In fact, the penguins' ancestors did fly, and today's penguins are highly specialized for life in a harsh environment. Penguin behavior and physiology has evolved to allow these handsome birds to thrive in a place where there is little other life.

© G. L. Kooyman/ Animals, Animals

*L*ike most birds, gentoo penguins look a little haggard while molting (opposite page).
. . . .

*M*ajestic king penguins, like penguins who live closer to the Antarctic, have trouble staying cool when the temperature rises too far above freezing.
. . . .

CHAPTER 2

THE LIFE OF A PENGUIN

*I*t's difficult to describe the life cycle of a "typical" penguin, since there are eighteen penguin species and despite many similarities, they all have different ways of mating, breeding, raising their young, and living their lives. Different species also live in different parts of the world in very different environments.

With that caveat, this chapter will describe, in simplified terms, the life of the Adélie penguin, not because it represents most penguins, but because the Adélie has been, until very recently, the most extensively studied and is the most well known penguin, both to scientists and the general public. Often researchers describe other species in comparison to the Adélie; when most people think of the "typical" penguin, with its crisp tuxedo and human waddle, they're thinking of the Adélie.

IN THE BEGINNING: MATING

The Adélie is one of the most southerly penguins; it lives around the South Pole on the Antarctic continent and its fringe islands. To the human eye, there's little difference between the males and females. The males are often heavier and have larger bills, but the only real way to tell them apart (besides by dissection) is to watch their display behavior, some of which is gender specific; watch them mate; or see who lays the eggs.

Adélies spend much of the year at sea, but at the beginning of the South Pole summer—around October—they migrate to land. They have an unerring ability to travel to the same place they mated the year before, which is often the place where they were born. In fact, they frequently end up on the exact same nest used the year before, and will vigorously defend it from would-be squatters. Scientists don't yet understand just how the penguin homing instinct works. There is speculation that it depends on the angle of the sun, but no one is completely sure.

Male Adélies arrive at the breeding grounds a few days before females. Because the

warmer weather is only beginning, there's still plenty of ice coming off the shore. Adélies will travel several days and up to forty miles (sixty-four kilometers) across ice to reach land. They can move as fast as humans through soft snow. They travel by walking, hopping, and sometimes by climbing, using their beaks as ice picks. They also "toboggan," flopping onto their bellies and pushing themselves along with their feet and wings.

Penguins travel together, often in long "trains." They avoid thin ice patches, which may break under their weight or harbor a leopard seal waiting to eat them. If there's no way around thin ice, the penguins will often wait a few hours until it freezes more thickly.

When they arrive at the nesting grounds, males will search for their old site, often digging it out of the snow, or will establish a new nest. There is fierce competition for nesting space, and frequently, fights break out between males. Once the nesting sites are established—and for some birds, especially younger ones, that may take a while—it's time to build the nests. This involves an intense hunt for suitable pebbles. Adélie nests are about fifteen inches (thirty-seven centimeters) across, shaped like saucers, and made only of pebbles. Pebble stealing is a continuous activity in penguin rookeries, and another source of fights. One researcher left a pile of specially colored pebbles in the middle of a penguin rookery to see how fast they would spread, and within a few days all the pebbles were evenly distributed throughout the colony.

After the males have been readying the nest site for a few days, the females arrive. Often the same male and female will mate across several years, and sometimes for life. But if a female is late to the rookery, the waiting male may be approached by a new prospective mate. There could be trouble if a female arrives to claim her old mate, only to find she's been replaced: the two females may fight it out.

Male penguins advertise their possession of a nest site and their availability as mates by

vocalizing and displaying. They point their bills to the sky, flap their flippers, and call loudly, in voices that no one would ever call melodious. Interested females may stop at the nest site, initiating a series of displays, may or may not result in the formulation of a pair bond. One common display is called the sideways stare (just what it sounds like); another involves bringing pebbles to a partner.

If a pair is formed, they will make quieter displays both together and alone. Birds younger than three years are not sexually mature but often form bonds and go through the motions of breeding, sometimes even incubating rocks. This "practice" nesting may improve their success when they are old enough to nest for real. However, such pairs usually split up in subsequent years, while mature pairs frequently nest together for several years in a row. Successful breeding does take some practice. Copulation in penguins

*W*eather can work against penguin nesting efforts, as this Adélie has discovered. If the inside of the nest is flooded, the eggs are doomed.
. . . .

© M. A. Chappell/Animals, Animals

somewhat resembles one football trying to balance on top of another. Much displaying usually precedes copulation, ensuring that male and female are synchronized and cooperating. The success of the mating effort won't be known until after the female has laid her eggs.

FROM EGGS TO CHICKS

Successful Adélies lay two eggs, one to four days apart, usually during the first two weeks of November. Incubation lasts roughly thirty-five days. After the second egg is laid, the male climbs on the nest and the female returns to the sea to feed. During the next three weeks, the male will fast.

On land, adult penguins have few predators. During the nesting season, however, eggs and small chicks are very vulnerable to predation from skuas, large gull-like birds with a voracious appetite for penguin eggs. Sometimes skuas will work in tandem to get an egg, one attacking the penguin and forcing him out of the nest while the other one swoops in to swipe the egg. Once the egg is out of the nest, the penguin will not retrieve it, even if he has a chance. This is true even if the egg rolls out by itself.

At any moment that the nest is unguarded, the eggs are vulnerable to skua attack. They're even vulnerable when the females return from

On land, penguins use their wings for balance when walking, for some forms of mating display, and sometimes for fighting.

© Dave Watts/Tom Stack & Associates

three weeks of feasting at sea to take their turn sitting on the nest. The switch must be made quickly, though it is accompanied by mutual bowing, humming, and other display behavior. For instance, often when a female returns to the nest, she'll present the male with a pebble. He may fetch one for her before he goes to sea in his turn to eat. The female will incubate the eggs for a week or so before the male returns, then both parents take regular turns until the chicks are born.

If an egg is snatched early in the breeding season, the penguin couple may lay another egg or two and incubate it until it hatches. Even if the later eggs manage to hatch, it's unlikely the chicks will survive to return to the sea with their older cousins several weeks

later. The Antarctic summer is only eight weeks long, and the penguin colony must move on schedule back into the sea. If some chicks haven't molted in time to take to the water, they are abandoned and likely to become food for a predator.

When chicks are born, their bodies are silver-gray and they have dark, nearly black heads. Their down isn't adequate protection from the cold, so they must stay snuggled under their parents. Chicks grow quickly, doubling their weight in their first two days and doubling it again in the next two days. They can often be seen with their bottoms and heads sticking out from under Mom or Dad. A parent must always be present; this is called the guard stage of chick rearing, and is

*A*délie parents take turns on the nest. One broods for several weeks while the other is at sea feasting, then they trade places. Adélie eggs need about five weeks to hatch.

© M. A. Chappell/Animals, Animals

This Adélie chick (far left) is nearing the time when he'll leave the nest and join other chicks in a kind of penguin daycare called the crèche stage of development.

*A*délie parents and chicks (near left) recognize each other by the sound of their voices. When parents bring food for the young, they listen for their offsprings' cries so they don't feed the wrong chick.

another time when the penguins are vulnerable to the skuas. Any unprotected chick is likely to be snatched and eaten alive.

After about three weeks, the chicks are old enough to leave the nest, but they can't fend for themselves yet. This is the beginning of the crèche stage, when the young chicks gather together in one part of the rookery. Some researchers say the crèche is like a nursery, with adult relatives watching over the chicks. Other researchers believe that the chicks are on their own, and that no adult protects them. Certainly the biggest advantage of the crèche is protection from cold and from skuas, the two biggest dangers to the young birds. There is strength in numbers. In bad weather, the chicks huddle together for warmth, and as long as they stay together, no skua will attack them. Any chick that wanders away from the crèche, however, is doomed.

While the chicks are in the crèche, the parents gather food. Penguins feed mostly on krill, small fish, squid, and crustaceans. They bring the food back to their chicks, who take if from their mouths. A parent penguin will feed only its own young, whom it identifies by the sound of its voice. Chicks know their parents' voices, and make a beeline for Mom or Dad as soon as they hear them.

But the parents don't just give the chicks their dinner. First they do a "feeding run." Mom or Dad alerts the chicks that it's time to eat, but as soon as the chicks approach, the parent runs away. The chicks give chase, and just as they've nearly caught up, Mom or Dad runs away again. Both chicks run after the parent, but usually one tires and lags behind and the other gets first dibs on the food. The second one will also be fed, but researchers speculate that the feeding run makes feeding easier since it prevents both chicks from clamoring for food at the same time. Parents with only one chick don't need to bother with a feeding run.

*A*délies
taking the plunge.
Usually one adventurous
penguin gets wet
first before the group
will follow.

. . . .

*W*hen they
first come to shore in the
summer, Adélies are plump
from months of ocean
feasting (opposite page).
They'll need the extra fat to
get them through several
weeks of fasting while they
brood.

. . . .

© Dave Watts/Tom Stack & Associates

INDEPENDENCE

By the beginning of February, the chicks are ready to feed themselves, and they move down to the water's edge. They can't swim yet, but they'll splash in the surf. They also practice climbing and play King of the Hill, competing with each other to stay on top of ice blocks. They'll even practice their climbing skills on accommodating Weddell seals.

By the end of February, or at latest the beginning of March, the penguins will return to the sea. The chicks brave the open water without help from adults, and their first swimming efforts are awkward. This is another time when the young birds are especially vulnerable, since there are likely to be leopard seals waiting offshore to make a meal of the penguins, and the inexperienced swimmers are the easiest ones to catch.

In the water, the young birds will learn several swimming styles. Underwater, they use their wings to propel themselves just like their cousins do in the air, "flying" at speeds of up to twenty-five miles (forty kilometers) per hour. They will also "porpoise" through the air, shooting up from the water and then diving back in. In addition, they'll learn a more restful swimming style that resembles the dog paddle. As with all other aspects of penguin life, they'll learn these swimming techniques, and all other survival skills they'll need, in the company of their many fellows. Penguins are nothing if not gregarious.

Their sociability is one of many intriguing features that make the penguins an especially successful species in the Southern Hemisphere. The next chapter will discuss those features in more detail.

CHAPTER · 3

PENGUIN PHYSIOLOGY

Most penguins, except those living in more northerly latitudes, not only live, but thrive in weather that would kill most other animals around the world. Again using the Adélie as an example of a "typical" penguin, let's look at some of the special features that have evolved in penguins to make them natural inhabitants of a forbidding place. Many people think the immediate problem facing penguins is the extreme cold of their environment. The subzero temperatures typical of Antarctic weather present a considerable challenge to humans; and like humans, penguins are warm-blooded. But penguins are well adapted to the cold. In fact, a bigger problem for them sometimes is coping with the heat, especially on those balmy summer days when the mercury climbs slightly above freezing.

*P*enguins
like these Adélies often
travel by riding ice floes.
. . . .

*P*enguins
live in one of the
globe's harshest yet most
intriguing environments
(opposite page). The
Antarctic's ice cap measures
two miles (3 km) deep, and
winter temperatures can be
colder than the
planet Mars.
. . . .

Just under the surface of their skin, penguins carry a thick insulating layer of blubber. It's as if they are wearing an internal wetsuit. The blubber also serves as a reserve of energy during breeding season, when penguins must fast for two or three weeks at a time and can lose up to 40 percent of their body weight.

On the outside, penguins have layers of remarkably efficient feathers. Next to the skin is a layer of down that keeps heat close to the body. The outer layer consists of feathers so numerous and tightly packed—up to three hundred per square inch—that they resemble scales. This feather layer is nearly impenetra- ble to wind and water. It is also more extensive than in any other bird. It even covers most of the upper part of an Adélie's bill. Heat escapes somewhat through the wings, or flippers, and through the feet and open beaks. Newly hatched chicks can't regulate their own body temperatures and rely on their parents to do it for them.

Even penguin feet are built for heat conservation. Getting blood to the brain and major muscles is a priority in the cold, and since a penguin's feet have no muscles, little blood is diverted to them. The feet, full of fat and tendons and covered by a thick skin, are con-

trolled by muscles in the fleshy part of the leg. In cold weather, the blood vessels of the feet contract to preserve heat.

There are two times when a penguin's feathers don't protect it against cold. Before a penguin chick has grown its first layer of adult, scalelike feathers, it can't survive in the water and will also be in trouble in severe storms, where the windchill can kill chicks who are only dressed in down. Similarly, an adult penguin can't go into the water when it is molting, since it is temporarily missing its insulating outer feather layer. Adélies molt once a year, just after mating season and before they return to the sea.

All this heat-retaining efficiency works to a penguin's detriment on a warm day, or after considerable exertion. When the sun shines in the Antarctic, hundreds of penguins can be seen holding their wings away from their bodies and panting with their mouths open and tongues out. The heat is especially hard on the chicks, who will lie flat on the ground on their bellies with their feet straight out behind them, soles up. In warm weather, the blood vessels in the feet expand and carry heat away from the body.

DIVING AND "FLYING" ADAPTATIONS

Once in the sea, penguins use their strong wings to move quickly through the water. In fact, though penguins are thought of as flightless birds, they move through water the same way aerial birds move through air. Penguins flap their wings and use their feet and tail for steering. Their wing muscles and connecting tendons are much stronger than those of aerial birds, and that makes sense, since penguins "fly" through a medium that is much heavier than air. Furthermore, the scalelike feathers reduce drag in the water.

Penguin bones are generally heavier than those of other birds, since being too buoyant in the water would make it difficult to dive at all. But penguins aren't too heavy, since that would make it difficult to stay on the surface. In fact, penguins weigh only about as much as the water they displace, which means there's a happy balance between weight and lightness that works to the penguin's advantage.

All penguins are both flightless (in air) and specialized for diving, and in this way are unique in the bird kingdom. Generally, penguins don't have to dive too deeply for their food, since most of it lives in the upper layers of the ocean. An average dive lasts about a minute, though emperor penguins have been observed in eighteen-minute dives (thought to be very rare).

There are at least three conditions that the penguin's body must take into account when diving. First, he must have an adequate supply of oxygen to dive down and come back up to the surface. Second, there must be a way to balance the increased water pressure against his body. And last, he must regulate his body temperature for the colder, deeper water.

The easiest way for a penguin to cope with these problems is to make shallow, quick dives. But if they need to make deeper dives, the chemistry of their blood helps them maintain necessary oxygen levels. All diving birds have more blood in their system and more oxygen in their blood than birds that don't dive, and in penguins, their lungs and air sacs also hold more oxygen. And a penguin's heart rate changes during a dive, going from approximately ninety beats a minute to twenty beats a minute. This is another way to conserve oxygen.

And, of course, penguins surface for air regularly. But they don't just pop their heads out of the water and take a deep breath. Penguins get their air by getting up to a good swimming ("flying") speed and then shooting out of the water. They coast along in the air for several

yards, then dive back down. While they're out of the water, they breathe rapidly to replace their oxygen, then exhale before diving. Penguins traveling any distance in the open sea usually combine underwater flying with porpoising, in what some researchers think is a way of saving energy. It's easier to travel by coasting through the air once in a while, rather than just flying through the water. In addition, they needn't stop moving to breathe.

When they dive, penguins are equipped to regulate increasing water pressure, but not to very great depths. Emperor penguins dive the deepest, and they go down about two hundred fifty yards (225m). If penguins dove deeper, they would probably get a bad case of the bends, which occur when the nitrogen content of the blood reaches dangerous levels.

As for keeping warm underwater, the feathers again play an important role, accounting for 80 percent of the bird's thermal insulation.

Though they seem awkward on land (left), penguins can travel up to 2.5 miles (3.9 km) an hour—about the speed of a walking human.

· · · · · · · · · · · ·

The imperial or blue-eyed shag (opposite page) dwells on the tip of South America and the Antarctic peninsula. It's neighbors include banded and Antarctic penguins.

· · · · · · · · · · · ·

The feathers trap air bubbles that work as added insulation underwater. During a dive, the bubbles get compressed, and after a long time underwater, a penguin will replace its feather air-bubble supply by preening.

BEING SOCIAL

Penguins have another adaptive process that helps keep them alive. They are extraordinarily social birds, and every aspect of penguin life is shared with thousands of other penguins. The birds migrate, mate, breed, raise their young, return to sea, and travel the southern oceans in huge flocks.

Besides providing company for each other—a somewhat unscientific explanation of penguin sociability—penguins derive distinct advantages from staying together. They usually huddle together in storms to stay warm. And their greater numbers make them a more formidable opponent for would-be predators. Penguins fall prey to skuas, leopard

*T*hese banded penguins (opposite page) are called blackfooted. Their interaction here might be playful, or a communication of mating status, or prelude to a fight.

. . . .

*T*aking a walk through a chinstrap colony.

. . . .

seals, and killer whales. They also fall prey to human beings and animals humans have introduced to the penguin environment, like dogs and rats. But the birds' natural predators rarely attack a bird that's surrounded by thousands of other birds, and will wait until a hapless penguin happens to be alone.

The social nature of these birds also allows them to take the fullest advantage of limited nesting space. Penguins build their nests very close to each other, so that a brooding parent is within bill's reach of his or her nearest neighbors. Close association helps in taking advantage of a localized food supply, as well.

It's also thought that penguins synchronize vital cycles like breeding in several ways, including stimulating each other through vocalizations. It's as if thousands of penguins who are newly arrived at their nesting sites hear a few loudmouthed penguins talking about raising a family, and follow their lead. Of course, no scientist would accept such an analogy—but it's hard not to think of penguins in anthropomorphic images.

Though all penguins are highly social, there is variety in behavior and physiology among different penguin species. The next chapter offers a look at the world's penguins.

King penguins (opposite page) at the beach. They live in southeast Australia, southwest New Zealand, and places of similar latitude.

. . . .

Chinstraps like to build nests on steep, rocky slopes.

. . . .

CHAPTER · 4

PENGUINS AROUND THE WORLD

*T*he scientific system of classification, invented by a Swedish botanist named Linnaeus in the 1700s, is used throughout the world to name every living organism known to humankind. According to the Linnaean system, all living matter fits several tiers of classification, going from most general to most specific. For instance, penguins belong to the class Aves, which includes all birds. They belong to the order Sphenisciformes and the family Spheniscidae, both of which are specific only to penguins. Within the penguin family there are six genera: *Aptenodytes, Pygoscelis, Magadyptes, Spheniscus, Eudyptes,* and *Eudyptula.* These genera hold all the species of penguin.

© Dave Watts/Tom Stack & Associates

*M*olting
Adélies share space with an emperor penguin (above). Often two or more penguin species will share territory on the edges of the Antarctic.

. . . .

*T*his
emperor penguin is molting (opposite page). Emperors, the world's largest penguins, can reach a height of four feet (1.2m) and weigh nearly 70 pounds (32kg).

. . . .

It's generally noted that there are eighteen penguin species, but in fact some scientists believe there are seventeen, or even sixteen; they put the little blue and the white-flippered penguins together, or consider some of the crested penguins to be subspecies of each other, rather than separate species. This chapter will consider each of the eighteen—or seventeen, or sixteen—species.

THE APTENODYTES

EMPERORS The scientific name of emperor penguins is *Aptenodytes forsteri*. They have more color than some of their cousins. Their beaks and heads have bold yellow markings, and the same color decorates their throat. At about four feet (1.2 meters), emperors are the largest penguins; a person crouching on the ground could look an emperor in the eye. At an average of sixty-six pounds (thirty kilograms), they're among the heaviest birds in the world. Depending on where they are in the mating or feeding sea-

son, their weight can range from forty to one hundred pounds (approximately twenty to forty-five kilograms).

Emperors are unique among penguins for two reasons. First, they never come to land—they breed on Antarctic shelf ice and spend the rest of the year at sea. Second, their breeding season is in the winter, when temperatures can drop to minus 150 degrees Fahrenheit (–101° Celsius). In fact, emperors are the only Antarctic birds that breed in winter. Scientists speculate this is a result both of ice movement and the birds' size: larger birds need more time to incubate, grow, and reach their first molt. Chicks must be ready to take to the water in time for the Antarctic's short summer, when food is most plentiful, so they must meet the world in the dead of winter.

There are twenty-three known emperor rookeries, all of which are found on ice surrounding the Antarctic continent. Eggs are laid in early June, and hatch in early August. Males come to the rookeries before the females, and last for a month or so before the females arrive. After eggs are laid—only one per couple—the males continue to fast as they incubate their offspring.

Since they breed and nest on ice, emperors don't make nests. They incubate the egg by holding it on top of their feet and wrapping it in a feathery flap of abdominal skin.

While the male takes the first incubation shift, the female returns to the sea. She will relieve her partner at about the time their chick is born. She then feeds the chick with regurgitated food, while the male, now quite thin, goes to sea for some well-deserved food.

Since their first layer of down can't protect them from the cold, emperor chicks stay on their parents' feet in the shelter of the abdominal flap for their first week and a half of life. By the time they're two months old, the chicks have gained some independence, though they still rely on their parents for food. Unlike other young penguins, who don't take to the water until after they molt into waterproof feathers, emperor chicks go

*K*ing penguin parents and their chick. Unlike some other penguins, kings lay only one egg in a mating cycle, and the chick doesn't venture on its own until it's a year old.

to sea while they're still clothed in downy feathers. They float away on broken pieces of ice. They don't actually spend time *in* the water, however, until after their first molt. When they reach adulthood, emperors can dive to depths of 1,000 feet (300 meters).

KINGS King penguins, *Aptenodytes patagonicus,* have markings similar to emperors, but they weigh in at about half the size. Their breeding grounds are north of the Antarctic, in the warmer climates of southeast Australia, southwest New Zealand, and places of similar latitude. A few have been reported on the Falkland Islands. Like emperors, kings lay a single egg. King rookeries are always near open waters, so the males and females have shorter and more frequent turns with incubation and rearing responsibilities.

In contrast to emperors and most other penguins, king chicks don't leave the rookeries for the first time until they are at least a year old. This means that kings have a different mating cycle than other penguins. They breed twice in three years, and not always at the same time of year. Because of this, king colonies show a greater range in ages than is usually seen in penguin colonies. For instance, at some times of year a rookery will be home to mating pairs, young birds in first molt and older molting birds, incubating eggs, and newly hatched chicks.

THE PYGOSCELIS

GENTOOS Gentoo penguins (*Pygoscelis papua*) have the distinctive marking of a white band that looks like a bonnet, stretching from eye to eye and widest at the crown of the head. In contrast to Adélies, gentoo beaks are yellow and not covered with feathers. The gentoos share their genus with Adélies and chinstrap penguins, but are bigger than these other species. All three penguin species, however, have breeding grounds that overlap, though gentoos aren't found as far south as chinstraps or Adélies. Sometimes an observer can see all three species nesting side by side. Gentoos mostly nest on or near territory along the outer reaches of the Antarctic. This is a border region called the Antarctic Convergence, where the water near the surface of the ocean is warmer than that nearer the Antarctic continent.

The gentoo mating season starts in mid-August in the north and mid-October in southern habitats. At least among some gentoos, the male doesn't show up alone to get the nest ready. Rather, the mating couple arrives as a pair and has presumably spent the previous season traveling the seas together. Though males initiate nest building, females also participate. They use pebbles, but also use bones, seaweed, moss, and grass. They like to build their nests on relatively level ground.

Gentoos lay two eggs, though on rare occasions scientists have seen them incubating four at a time. The extra eggs are probably from another female. Chicks hatch in about three weeks. They stay in the nest until they're about five weeks old, then move into a crèche with other young gentoos. During the crèche stage, the young birds huddle together for warmth and protection, and await food from a parent. Their meals consist more of small fish and squid and krill. One result of this diet is the color of their droppings, which tend to be white. Penguins who eat more krill, like the Adélies and chinstraps, leave pink droppings.

Gentoos have been described as the most timid penguins, and have been known to desert a nest rather than defend it.

CHINSTRAPS This penguin earned its name from the telltale "strap" of white that circles under its chin, from cheek to cheek. Its head, back, and beak are black. Chinstraps are more aggressive penguins.

Their mating sites are close to those of the Adélie, though they don't cover as wide an area, nor are they found as far south. Unlike the gentoo and Adélie, which prefer flat land for nests, chinstraps like to nest on steep,

It's obvious where chinstrap penguins get their name.

47

*B*ecause of special glands that secrete excess salt, penguins like this chinstrap may drink salt water with no harmful effects.

rocky slopes. That isn't a hard-and-fast rule, however, since there are some large colonies on flat shores.

Chinstraps arrive at their rookeries at different times, depending on how far south or north the breeding site is. On average, mating season begins in early or mid-November, initiated by mating behavior similar to that of the Adélie. Nest building, however, is a much simpler affair. Sometimes chinstraps' nests are only a handful of pebbles, just enough to prevent the eggs from rolling away. After the eggs are laid—there are usually two—the males return to sea for several days. The females fast for about a month. Then the mates relieve each other from incubation duty every few days.

Hatching time varies with the rookery's latitude, but chicks poke through their shells around mid-January, after an average of five weeks' incubation. There's not much hard data on how long the brooding stage lasts, but all chinstraps clear out of their rookeries between late March and late April.

ADÉLIES Adélies, or *Pygoscelis adeliae,* are the world's best-known penguins. The white markings around their eyes make them look like clowns, and their body markings, like other Antarctic penguins', make them look like they're dressed for opening night at the opera. Adélies, like most penguins, are gregarious birds, and are very inquisitive. Visitors to the Antarctic have reported Adélies who walk right up to them, almost as if to say hello. Though they're not afraid of humans, Adélies can be as defensive as chinstraps if they feel threatened.

Adélies share their territories with emperors and the other *Pygoscelis* penguins, though their range, along with that of the emperors, is the most southerly of any penguin. They eat mostly krill and small fish.

Since Adélies are often used as examples when discussing penguins in general, they have been described in some detail in the second part of Chapter 1 and throughout Chapter 2. The reader is referred there for more information.

*H*umboldts, or Peruvian penguins, live on the coasts of Peru and Chile. They are better adapted to heat than their Antarctic cousins— note the area around the beak without feathers.

THE SPHENISCUS

MAGELLANIC, Humboldt, Galapagos and Black-footed. Because of their markings, these birds are known collectively as the banded penguins. The four species are so similar that scientists assume they diverged from a common ancestor relatively recently. The black-footed and Humboldt penguins have been familiar in zoos for years, but not much is known about the habits of banded penguins in the wild.

These birds breed farther north than some of their *Pygoscelis* and *Aptenodytes* kin. They are found in South America, the Falkland Islands, and off the coasts of Peru, Chile, and Argentina. Though they live in more temperate climates, the banded penguins are still sensitive to heat. Scientists speculate that heat regulation is one reason the banded penguins build their nests by burrowing into the ground.

Magellanic penguins, *Spheniscus magellanicus,* generally live on islands at the tip of South America, usually on islands, though there are large coastal colonies farther north. They lay eggs in early October, in burrow-nests or under bushes. Hatching begins in mid-November. The chicks grow more slowly than the other banded penguins. They fledge, or molt for the first time, at about three months. Magellanics stay at their breeding site for much of the year, and go to sea for the rest.

Humboldt penguins, *Spheniscus Humboldti,* are also called Peruvian penguins. They are better adapted to heat than some other penguins, since they have more unfeathered skin around their eyes. They share some breeding space with the Magellanics off the coast of Chile, but the two species use the habitats at different times. Humboldts are distinguishable from Magellanics because, instead of double black bands, Humboldts have only one band running across their chests.

It's estimated that there are only 20,000 Humboldts left in the world, though they once numbered in the hundreds of thousands. On some islands of Peru, their guano was reported to be up to one hundred meters thick. The guano was a rich fertilizer, and made Humboldts commercially profitable. But their numbers have been shrinking due to a number of reasons: the guano harvest disrupts breeding; the primary food sources, anchovettas, have been overfished; and the recent El Niño was responsible for a high mortality rate.

The Galapagos penguins, *Spheniscus mendiculus,* are the most tropical penguins in the world. They live at the equator, on the Galapagos Islands, as their name implies. The dense feather coverings of their Antarctic kin would prove a severe disadvantage in such a warm climate; Galapagos penguins have large areas of skin exposed on their faces so that they won't overheat. They use the coolest waters available for swimming and foraging; water located in the western part of the Galapagos

*G*alapagos penguins live where their name suggests. Theirs is the world's warmest penguin habitat, as the presence of a fellow island-dweller suggests.

© G. L. Kooyman/Animals, Animals

The black-footed penguin (right) is a close cousin to the similarly marked Humboldt penguin.

Yellow-eyed penguins (opposite page), found in New Zealand, differ from other penguins in their markings and migrating habits. They're also the most endangered penguin species.

Islands is generally cooler than water around much of the rest of the equator.

At mating season, Galapagos penguins prefer to find ready-made nests in lava cracks instead of burrowing. Eggs are mostly laid in August and September, but Galapagos penguins breed throughout the year. Males and females switch places on the nest as often as every other day. Chicks hatch after about six weeks. Like Antarctic penguins, Galapagos penguins are responsible for their chicks' thermoregulation during the first weeks of life. In this case, however, the challenge is to keep the chicks cool. Chicks fledge at about two months. The Galapagos are unique among all penguins in that they molt twice a year, rather than just once. They also have a more varied diet than most penguins.

Black-footed penguins, *Spheniscus demersus,* are the only banded penguins who live

off the tip of South Africa. They so closely resemble Humboldts that it's hard to tell them apart, except that Humboldts are not found in South Africa. Black-footed penguins live close to a major shipping lane, and often pay the prices of oil spills and other problems that humans introduce into the environment.

THE MEGADYPTES

There is only one penguin in this genus, and that's the yellow-eyed penguin, *Megadyptes antipodes,* of New Zealand. It's fitting that this bird has its own genus, since it differs from its fellow penguin species in several important ways.

First, the yellow-eyed penguins live in small groups. Isolated males will walk more than a mile from shore to meet mates, who have also traveled to the mating ground alone. Nests are built in protected niches on the ground, out of sight and earshot of any neighbors. When chicks have been reared and are ready for the sea, they venture there alone. This is in stark contrast to the raucous and crowded scene at most penguin rookeries, when thousands of newly fledged chicks take the plunge en masse.

The yellow-eyeds' markings are a second unique trait. Their head is crowned with yellow, and their eyes—not just the markings around the eyes, but the eyes themselves—are yellow.

Yellow-eyeds are also unusual because of their migratory habits: they have none. Most birds spend their lives in the same places where they breed and raise young.

Lastly, yellow-eyeds are currently in more danger of extinction than any other penguin species. Their New Zealand habitat is in an area heavily populated by humans, and humans have brought predators into the area that are doing a good job of reducing yellow-eyed populations. We'll discuss this in more detail in the last chapter.

THE EUDYPTES

ROYAL, Snares Island, Fjordland, Erect-crested, Rockhopper, Macaroni.

The birds of this genus are called crested penguins because of the gold plumes they all carry on their heads. The Snares Island penguins are found only on the New Zealand island of the same name, and royal penguins are found only on Macquarie Island, also in New Zealand. The Fjordland and erect-crested penguins are the two other *Eudyptes* found exclusively in New Zealand. Rockhoppers live throughout the area between the Antarctic and subtropical convergences. Macaroni penguins are found on many of the subantarctic islands, and sometimes share nesting grounds with chin strap penguins.

Like the banded penguins, the crested penguins evolved away from each other only recently, and the six different species have very similar markings; to the untrained eye, it's often difficult to tell them apart. In fact, they're so close that some researchers think perhaps there aren't six species, but only five. If this were so, the macaroni and royal penguins would be considered members of the same species. Or, say another camp of scientists, perhaps the Snares Island and Fjordland penguins ought to be grouped together. Most students of penguins, however, consider the six groups separate species.

Crested penguins share some physical characteristics, but their habitats, breeding cycles, and nesting sites vary greatly. Some build nests of pebbles, others use grass and twigs, others simply use the ground they stand on as

nests. Most of the crested penguins, however, share an odd reproduction habit. They usually lay two eggs, but the first is always smaller than the second, and is discarded shortly after incubation begins. The second egg will be nurtured to hatching. No one is quite sure why this happens.

Some species of crested penguins are better represented than others. For example, as of 1984, there were 2.5 million royal penguins (*Eudyptes schlegeli*) in the world. Gender difference is clearer on royals than on some penguins; the female has a shorter, thinner beak and a gray face, compared to a male's white face. Mating season starts in mid-September, with egg laying a month later. The males and females take two-week turns on the nest; the female broods first. Though the couple lays two eggs, only one will hatch, sometime after the middle of November. Males stay with the chick while females keep the food supply plentiful. Males return to the sea after the chicks join a crèche. In late January, the chicks go to sea with the adults, but the adults return after five weeks to molt. All the royals are gone from the island by the end of March.

Like royals, Snares Island penguins (*Eudyptes robustus*) only live in one place in the world, the islands for which they're named. There are about 135 colonies on the islands, with a total of between 30,000 and 50,000 birds. The Snares Islanders look like Fjord land penguins, except they have paler skin around their beaks and they have no stripes on their cheeks. Their breeding cycle starts the same time as the royals', and has a similar rhythm.

The other two New Zealand–specific penguins are the Fjordlands (*Eudyptes pachyrhynchus*) and the erect-cresteds (*Eudyptes sclateri*). Fjordlands are called such because they breed in rain forest fjords on the southwest of New Zealand's South Island, and on smaller islands to the south. Fjordlands have gray feathers at the base of their cheeks, and when they ruffle their feathers, their faces look mottled. They come to their rookeries in

© Kjell B. Sandved

*I*t's clear why macaroni penguins are classified with the crested penguins. Macaronis live in islands off the Antarctic peninsula and the southern tip of Africa.

early July to mate and lay eggs. Usually, they return to the same nest and same mate they used the year before. There may be barnacles growing on their tails when they first come to shore, a sure sign they've been at sea awhile.

The erect-crested penguins also have rookeries on South Island and on other islands south of New Zealand. These birds are slightly larger than Snares Island and Fjordland penguins. Sailors shipwrecked off South Island in 1893 were probably the first Westerners to meet erect-crested penguins. They owed their lives to the birds, since they lived off roast penguin and scrambled penguin eggs for the eighty-seven days they were stranded.

All the penguins of New Zealand were quite familiar to the indigenous people of New Zealand, the Maori. Today, however, there are few Maori in southern New Zealand, and the Maori names for some of the penguins have been lost.

Rockhopper penguins (*Eudyptes crestatus*) breed in New Zealand, but they're also found on the Falkland Islands and farther south on islands just outside the Antarctic Convergence. These hardy penguins aren't the smallest crested penguins, but at an average height of two feet (sixty centimeters), they're the smallest penguins who live so close to the Antarctic.

© Kjell B. Sandved

Their name derives from the unusual way they get around on land: they hop. And they don't hop where it's easy to hop: they hop on steep, rocky, wave-battered shores and up craggy slopes. Rockhoppers can hop as high as a foot straight up, or half their height in a single bound. They use beaks, flippers, and sharp toenails to help themselves climb. And instead of diving into the water, as do all other penguin species, rockhoppers jump in feet-first.

Rockhopper rookeries are found on exposed beaches, where gale-force winds are the norm. One would think rockhopper eggs need special protection from the fierce elements, but rockhopper nests are monuments to minimalism. They are merely shallow furrows in the ground, dug within a beak's peck of neighboring nests. Nests are built—or rather, scraped—in early October with the first arrival of the males. Females join their mates two weeks later.

Egg laying begins in early November. Like macaroni and royal penguins, rockhopper females do their first stint of incubating before the males. This is uncommon, because among most penguins, it is the male's responsibility to incubate the eggs first.

Eggs start hatching in early December. After ten weeks, chicks and adults leave the rookery. Adults return to molt after a few weeks of feasting at sea, and then leave the rookery for the winter by late April.

No penguin has a melodious call, at least to human ears, but the rockhopper's cry has elicited a particularly evocative description. British ornithologist Robin Wood said they sound like "a rusty wheelbarrow pushed along too fast," and was quite impressed with the cacophonic symphony of a rockhopper rookery.

Last but not least of the crested penguins are the macaronis (*Eudyptes chysolophus*). They live on islands off the Antarctic peninsula and the southern tip of Africa. A few have also been found on the Falklands. In some places, their breeding grounds overlap those of the chinstrap. There are plenty of macaronis in the world; one estimate says there are as many as 40 million.

Macaronis arrive to breed in mid-September in some rookeries, and in late October or early November in others. Nests

*L*eopard
seals (right) love to
munch on penguins. Young
birds venturing into
the water for the first
time are an especially
easy—and delectable—
catch.
. . . .

*L*ittle blues,
also called fairy
penguins,
are the smallest
penguins (opposite page).
They are native to New
Zealand and southern
Australia.
. . . .

are made by scraping gravelly or sandy ground and lining the depression with stones, grass, and/or sand. The females incubate the eggs first, for about two weeks. The chicks hatch after about five weeks and leave the rookery after about sixty-five days.

Macaronis are known to be noisy and aggressive. They don't hop, but move across land like *Pygoscelis* penguins.

THE EUDYPTULA

LITTLE BLUE, WHITE-FLIP-PERED
The little blues (*Eudyptula minor*) and white-flippered penguins were once considered separate species, the latter holding the scientific name *Eudyptula albosignata*. Today, however, the white-flippered penguin is classified by most researchers as a local sub-species of the little blue. Here they will be discussed as one species.

The little blues, also called fairy penguins, get their name from the bluish sheen of their feathers. They are the smallest of all penguins, sometimes tipping the scales at no more than a pound and a half (less than one kilogram). They live in New Zealand and southern Australia. They congregate in colonies like most penguins, but they seem to like their privacy; nests are built far apart. Nests consist of burrows, sometimes up to three feet (.9 meter) deep, lined with grass and twigs. Little blues spend some time at sea, but usually stay close to their nesting grounds.

Mating season starts around late July, and eggs are laid from mid-August to mid-September. There are two eggs, and most hatch in October and November. Oddly, after the chicks are two days old, little blues feed them only in the evening. And often one chick will manage to get four to eight times as much food as his or her sibling.

For the first two or three weeks of life, chicks are constantly guarded by one or both parents. At about the third week, only one

parent looks after the chick, and then only at night. By the fourth week, a chick is left completely unattended. These penguins don't have a crèche stage, when all the chicks gather together for a few weeks. When they are eight or ten weeks old, the chicks will head for the sea.

PREDATION

This chapter hasn't mentioned penguin predators. Since the penguins themselves vary tremendously in their ranges, breeding cycles, mating habits, and general life patterns, it makes sense that their natural predators are also varied. They range from leopard seals, skua, and giant petrels to sea lions, wekas (a flightless New Zealand land bird), and elephant seals.

But by far the most menacing and increasingly the most prevalent penguin predator is humankind. The next chapter will explore the ever more delicate balance that must be met between human needs for growth and resources and penguin needs for space, a pollution-free environment, and an adequate food supply.

CHAPTER 5

HUMANS AND PENGUINS: A FRAGILE HARMONY

*T*he history of penguin-human relations has been strained from the start. When the men of Vasco da Gama's expedition sighted penguins in 1497, it was noted "we killed as many as we chose." Antonio Pigafetta, the meticulous observer accompanying Magellan's 1520 voyage, wrote of penguins, "They were so fat that we did not pluck them, but skinned them." It's not unreasonable that the men on these ships provided themselves with food from the local fauna. But men sailing with Francis Drake in 1578

*G*entoo chicks, like most young penguins, depend on their parent for all their food until the entire colony returns to the sea sometime in late February.

wrote, "We killed in less than one day 3000 and victualed ourselves thoroughly there-with.... To take them we had staves with hookes fast to the ends, wherewith some of our men pulled them out and others being ready with cudgels did knocke them on the head." And in 1594, a sailor reported, "The hunting [of penguins] was a great recreation to my company and worth the sight ... in getting them once within the Ring, few escaped ... and there was no drove which yeelded us not a thousand." (These quotes are drawn from George Simpson's excellent 1984 book, *Penguins: Past and Present, Here and There.*)

THE SAGA CONTINUES

As more people and more sophisticated technology followed these early discoveries, penguins only fared worse, especially when it was discovered that they had commercial value. Penguin fat was used for fuel, penguin down stuffed pillows, penguin skin became gloves and hats, and penguin droppings became garden fertilizer.

As the great whaling and sealing industries moved into the Antarctic and surrounding waters, penguins were not spared. In New Zealand, huge vats of boiling oil were set up near rookeries, and hapless penguins were driven alive into the cookers. Supposedly, king penguins were obliterated from the Falkland Islands when the last of them was turned into roof sealant.

By far the worst direct exploitation of most penguins has come from egg harvests. Three hundred thousand black-footed penguin eggs are sold every year on Dassen Island, off the South African coast. In the Falkland Islands a national egg day—November 9—was a school holiday, and people collected thousands and thousands of eggs from penguin nests. Falkland Islanders like penguin eggs year-

© Kjell B. Sandved

round, however, and once ate an average of more than sixty eggs per person every year. The eggs that became breakfast were mostly from rockhoppers, though Magellanics were also represented. Penguin colonies near the town of Port Stanley, the only town on the Falklands, were wiped out. Today, Falkland Islanders still eat penguin eggs, but not as many. About 10,000 eggs a year are collected, but the penguins are at least given a chance to replenish their clutch.

Today, all Antarctic penguins are protected by the 1959 Antarctic Treaty, which prohibits exploitation and molestation of all Antarctic birds and mammals. But that doesn't mean all penguins are protected, nor that the Antarctic birds don't suffer ill effects from human influence. Humans have introduced new predators into Antarctic territories; penguins have no defense against dogs and rats. And though people can't kill penguins as they please anymore, there are more and more people every year who travel to the Antarctic as tourists; last year there were more than a thousand.

These magellanic penguins on the Falkland Islands look like they're in procession. Because of their markings, magellanics are known as banded penguins.

*L*ike all
their cousin penguin
species, gentoos are highly
social birds. No part of a
gentoo penguin's life is lived
in solitude, just as no act
is performed alone.

. . . .

*K*ing
penguins look like
emperors, but they live in a
warmer climate. They're
about half the size and
weight of their larger
cousins.

. . . .

*Y*ellow-eyed
penguins cross nearly a mile
(1.6km) of land (opposite
page) to find their secluded
nesting sites. When they're
ready to leave the nest,
they go to sea alone.

. . . .

Even scientists cause problems. Two thousand researchers live in Antarctica every summer, and eight hundred stay the year. It's been shown that research stations set up near penguin colonies have a deleterious effect on the birds. In some places, especially where research stations have been long established, penguin populations have been nearly halved. This doesn't mean scientists are bludgeoning or persecuting penguins like their sixteenth-century explorer forebears. But their impact on the environment can have the same effect: penguins die.

Outside Antarctica, birds compete with humans for living space. In New Zealand, for instance, yellow-eyed penguins once freely roamed the southeast coast of South Island. Now they're confined to a piece of coastal forest less than half a mile long. First farmers and then other land developers have encroached on the yellow-eyed habitat. Today there is an 85 percent chance that young yellow-eyeds won't reach breeding age. Many are killed by predators introduced into their environment, like cats and feral pigs. But increasingly, yellow-eyed penguins are simply starving to death. Experts estimate there are only 1,400 breeding pairs of yellow-eyeds left in the world.

LARGER PROBLEMS

For a long time, the Antarctic was considered the least polluted place on earth—but that is changing. Ships that bring scientists and tourists dump tons of trash overboard every year. Though tourists often just want a photo of themselves amid a penguin colony to show the folks back home, these seemingly innocent forays into rookeries cause long-lasting damage. Penguins approached by humans often desert their nests, leaving their eggs for a skua's supper.

Much of the garbage will not biodegrade. The scientists live in more than fifty different research stations, generating yet more refuse. And none of the stations has facilities for dealing with sewage.

In February 1989, an Argentine freighter spilled oil off the coast of the Antarctic peninsula, decimating penguin and skua rookeries. One researcher familiar with the affected penguin rookeries described a gruesome scene of oil-coated birds eating their own young, utterly confused about what was food and what was family after the oil destroyed their sense of smell.

One may argue that an oil spill, though tragic, is an isolated event, yet Argentine tankers alone cause frequent oiling problems along the coast. Other influences are even less isolated and more insidious. Humans have discovered that krill is a good source of food, and have recently begun harvesting tremendous amounts of it from the ocean. Miles-wide nets are dragged, capturing tons and tons of krill. This punches holes in the krill supply that ocean animals depend on for survival, and some scientists are concerned that unlimited

© William E. Larose/GreenPeace

human exploitation of krill will mean other creatures starve for lack of it.

There are even influences from above the earth. The ozone layer, a band of air in the upper atmosphere, blocks some of the sun's ultraviolet radiation. Atmospheric scientists have been warning since the mid-1970s that the ozone layer is being depleted by hazardous chemicals, especially the chlorofluorocarbons used in refrigerants and aerosols. When the ozone layer develops holes, the earth—and all that lives on it—is exposed to more ultraviolet radiation than it can naturally handle. The ever-growing ozone hole over the South Pole presently covers an area about the size of the United States.

The results of excessive exposure to ultraviolet, or UV, radiation have yet to be fully understood, but already scientists see signs of trouble. For example, too much UV radiation means Antarctic plants and organisms at the bottom of the food chain, like phytoplankton, don't convert sunlight into energy the way they should. As a result, there is a smaller food supply at the very link of the food chain that must provide the most food. Krill feed on phytoplankton, and everything from whales to penguins to squid feeds on krill.

SIGNS OF HOPE

Clearly, the problems confronting penguins and Antarctica at large will not be solved overnight. But for the last thirty years, a treaty has been in place that at least ensures the problems will be addressed. The Antarctic Treaty of 1959, ultimately signed by eighteen nations and agreed to by sixteen more, calls for scientific stewardship of the continent that comprises a tenth of the world's land. The treaty banned military activity, stopped territorial claims, and set aside Antarctica as a nuclear-free zone. It allowed any nation to conduct scientific research, as long as other nations could see the results.

The treaty is due to be reconsidered in 1991, at which time any participating nation can withdraw. New claims are being made on Antarctica. Energy-hungry nations want to explore the continent for oil, even though researchers with the U.S. Geological Survey assert there are no known petroleum resources there. Others see Antarctica as the perfect place to dump nuclear and toxic wastes or the ideal place to store excess food. And still other countries want a way to take advantage of the frozen fresh water trapped in the continent; by some estimates, it holds three-quarters of all the fresh water in the world.

This well-fed gentoo chick may become a rare sight if penguin habitats continue to be destroyed.

A hillside covered in green (right) near this chinstrap colony is an unusual sight, even in the Antarctic summer, when the temperature barely warms up to freezing.

. . . .

*T*his gentoo parent might be off for food for the chicks. It's nearly impossible to tell male and female penguins apart, except during mating season, when certain display behavior meant to win a mate is gender-specific (opposite page).

. . . .

Thus far, saner heads prevail in the struggle for the only unpoliticized, unowned piece of the globe. But precious resources like fresh water and energy supplies are running low in the rest of the world. Those who would protect and preserve Antarctica face an increasingly heated battle to keep the last unspoiled continent from becoming the next exploited continent.

Penguins don't have much to say as the debate intensifies, but those who know and admire penguins can say much on their behalf. George Simpson, a penguin researcher for several decades, says it well.

The question may be asked, "What good are penguins?"... That depends on what you mean by good. If you mean "good to eat," you are perhaps being stupid. If you mean "good to hunt," you are surely being vicious. If you mean "good as it is good in itself to be a living creature enjoying life," you are not being crass, stupid, or vicious. I agree with you, and I am your brother as well as the penguin's.

Useful References
For More Information On Penguins

Austin, Oliver J., ed. 1968. *Antarctic Bird Studies.*
   Baltimore: Horn-Shafer. National Academy of Sciences/
   National Research Council, Publication No. 1686.

Croxall, J.P., ed. 1987. *Seabirds: Feeding Ecology and Role in Marine Ecosystems.*
   Cambridge, England: Cambridge University Press.

Levick, G.M. 1914. *Antarctic Penguins.* London: Heinemann.

Matthews, L. Harrison. 1978. *Penguins, Whalers, and Sealers: A Voyage of Discovery.*
   New York: Universe Books.

Muller-Schwarze, Dietland. 1984. *The Behavior of Penguins: Adapted to Ice and
   Tropics.* Albany, NY: State University of New York Press.

Peterson, Roger Tory. 1979. *Penguins.* Boston: Houghton Mifflin.

Pettingill, E.R. 1960. *Penguin Summer.* London: Cassell.

Simpson, George Gaylord. 1976. *Penguins: Past and Present, Here and There.*
   New Haven: Yale University Press.

Stonehouse, B. 1968. *Penguins.* New York: Golden Press.

Watson, George E. 1975. *Birds of the Antarctic and Sub-Antarctic.* Washington:
   American Geophysical Union.

Sober, Tony and Sparks, John. 1987. *Penguins.* New York: Facts on File, Inc.

Index

A

Adélie penguins
  Antarctic habitat, 24
  classification and
    characteristics, 49
  eggs, 27–28
  humans' effect on, 17
  mating and breeding,
    24–29
  naming of, 16
  nesting, 25
  predators, 27–28
  as "typical" penguin, 24
Antarctic, 24, 28–55, 63–64
Antarctic Treaty (1959), 63,
  66–67

B

Black-footed penguins, 16,
  52
Blubber, 16, 34
Bones, 37
Breeding. *See* Mating and
  breeding

C

Cavendish, Thomas, 14
Chicks
  feeding, 29
  heat conservation in,
    34–36
  independence, 30
  rearing of, 28–29
  swimming, 30
Chinstrap penguins, 17,
  47–49
Classification, 43–44
Cook, James, 14
Crested penguins, 54–58

D

da Gama, Vasco, 14, 61
Diet, 29
Displaying, in mating, 25
Diving, wing use in, 36–38
Drake, Francis, 14, 61–63
Dumont d'Urville, Jules
  Sebastien César, 16

E

Ecology, 64–66
Eggs, 16, 27–28, 63
Emperor penguins, 8, 14, 19,
  37, 44–46
Endangerment, 63–66
Environment. *See* Habitat
Erect-crested penguins, 55
Evolution, 19–20

F

Fairy penguins, 8, 58
Falkland Islands, 16, 55, 63
Feathers
  diving and, 37–38
  as insulation, 34
  molting, 36
Feet, physiology, 34–36
Fjordland penguins, 55
Forster, Johann Reinhold, 14
Fossils, 11, 19–20

G

Galapagos penguins, 51–52
Gentoo penguins, 17, 47

H

Habitat
  adaptation to, 33
  extent of, 8
  pre-historic, 20

as protected areas, 17
  southern hemisphere, 14
Heart rate, 37
Heat conservation, 34–36
Homing instinct, 24
Humboldt penguins, 50–51
Huxley, Thomas, 19

J

Jackass penguins. *See*
  Black-footed penguins

K

Killer whales, 41
King penguins, 16, 46

L

Leopard seals, 30, 38–41
Linnaeus, 43
Little blue penguins. *See*
  Fairy penguins
Locomotion, 25

M

Macaroni penguins, 57–58
Magellan, Ferdinand, 14
Magellanic penguins, 14,
  50–52
Maori people, 13, 55
Mating and breeding, 17,
  24–29, 41, 44–49, 57

N

Nesting, 41, 25
New Zealand, 19, 55

O

Oxygen levels, during diving,
  37

P

Patagonia, 14
Penguin, origin and use of
  word, 14
Physiology, 34–38
Pigafetta, Antonio, 14, 61
Pollution, 64–66
Predators, 27–28, 38–41, 58
  chicks and, 29

R

Rockhopper penguins, 55–57
Royal penguins, 55

S

Simpson, George, 63, 69
Skuas, 27–28, 29, 38
Snares Island penguins, 55
Sociability, 38–41
Southern hemisphere, 14
Species, number of, 11
Swimming, 30

V

Vocalizing, 41, 57
  in mating behavior, 25

W

Weddell seals, 30
White-flippered penguins,
  58
Wings, diving adaptation
  and, 36–38
Wood, Robin, 57

Y

Yellow-eyed penguins, 52